Angel Voic
Beautiful Poems of A

Compiled by Hugh Morrison

Montpelier Publishing
London
MMXV

ISBN-13: 978-1512355246
ISBN-10: 1512355240
Published by Montpelier Publishing, London.
Printed by Amazon Createspace.

Angels in the early morning

Angels in the early morning
May be seen the dews among,
Stooping, plucking, smiling, flying:
Do the buds to them belong?
Angels when the sun is hottest
May be seen the sands among,
Stooping, plucking, sighing, flying;
Parched the flowers they bear along.

Emily Dickinson

The Two Angels

God called the nearest angels who dwell with Him above:
The tenderest one was Pity, the dearest one was Love.
'Arise,' He said, 'my angels! a wail of woe and sin
Steals through the gates of heaven, and saddens all within.

'My harps take up the mournful strain that from a lost world swells,
The smoke of torment clouds the light and blights the asphodels.
'Fly downward to that under world, and on its souls of pain
Let Love drop smiles like sunshine, and Pity tears like rain!'

Two faces bowed before the Throne, veiled in their golden hair;
Four white wings lessened swiftly down the dark abyss of air.
The way was strange, the flight was long; at last the angels came
Where swung the lost and nether world, red-wrapped in rayless flame.

There Pity, shuddering, wept; but Love, with faith too strong for fear,
Took heart from God's almightiness and smiled a smile of cheer.
And lo! that tear of Pity quenched the flame whereon it fell,
And, with the sunshine of that smile, hope entered into hell!

Two unveiled faces full of joy looked up-ward to the Throne,
Four white wings folded at the feet of Him who sat thereon!
And deeper than the sound of seas, more soft than falling flake,
Amidst the hush of wing and song the Voice Eternal spake:

'Welcome, my angels! ye have brought a holier joy to heaven;
 Henceforth its sweetest song shall be the song of sin forgiven!'

John Greenleaf Whittier

A Song of Two Angels

Two angels came through the gate of Heaven.
(White and soft is a mother's breast!)
Stayed them both by the gate of Heaven;
Rested a little on folded wings,
Spake a little of holy things.
(In Heaven alone is perfect rest!)

Over them rose the golden steeps,
Heaven's castled and golden steeps;
Under them, depth on depth of space
Fell away from the holy place.

'Brother, and now I must take my way,
Glad and joyful must take my way,
Down to the realm of day and night;
Down to yon earth that rolls so bright.'

'Brother, I too am thither sent;
Sad and silent, am thither sent.
Let us together softly wing
Our flight to yon world of sorrowing.'

Down they swept through the shining air,
Swiftly sped through the shining air,—
This one bright as the sunset's glow,
That one white as the falling snow.

'Brother, and tell me your errand now!
Tell me your joyful errand now!'
 'A little new soul must wake on earth,
And I carry the blessing for its birth.'

'And tell me, brother, what task is yours?
Dear white angel, what task is yours?'
'To bear a soul back to Heaven's height,—
A mother, whose child is born to-night.'

'Ah! will the mother be sad to go?
Loath to leave her baby and go?'
 'Hush, dear angel! she will not know.
God in His mercy wills it so.'

'Ah! will the baby wake forlorn?
Seek its mother, and weep forlorn?'
'Hush, dear angel! we may not know.
God, knowing all things, wills it so.'

Down they swept through the dusky air
Swiftly sped through the dusky air;
Trod the dim earth with noiseless feet;
Softly stole through a village street.

Now they came to a cottage door,
Stayed them both at a cottage door,—
This one bright as the sunset's glow,
That one white as the falling snow.

'Brother, I trow we here must part!
Dear white angel, we here must part!
For this low door I must enter by.'
'Alas! and alas! so too must I!'

Sad they gazed in each other's face;
(White and soft is a mother's breast;)
Lingered and looked in each other's face;
Then folded their hands in silent prayer,
And so together they entered there.
(In Heaven alone is perfect rest.)

Laura Elizabeth Richards

Azrael

The angels in high places
Who minister to us,
Reflect God's smile,—their faces
Are luminous;
Save one, whose face is hidden,
(The Prophet saith),
The unwelcome, the unbidden,
Azrael, Angel of Death.
And yet that veilèd face, I know
Is lit with pitying eyes,
Like those faint stars, the first to glow
Through cloudy winter skies.

That they may never tire,
Angels, by God's decree,
Bear wings of snow and fire,—
Passion and purity;
Save one, all unavailing,
(The Prophet saith),
His wings are gray and trailing,
Azrael, Angel of Death.
And yet the souls that Azrael brings
Across the dark and cold,
Look up beneath those folded wings,
And find them lined with gold.

Robert Gilbert Welsh

'There Shall Be More Joy...'

The little angels of Heaven
Each wear a long white dress,
And in the tall arcadings
Play ball and play at chess;

With never a soil on their garments,
Not a sigh the whole day long,
Not a bitter note in their pleasure,
Not a bitter note in their song.

But they shall know keener pleasure,
And they shall know joy more rare—
Keener, keener pleasure
When you, my dear, come there.

The little angels of Heaven
Each wear a long white gown,
And they lean over the ramparts
Waiting and looking down.

Ford Madox Ford

Time and Eternity

God permits industrious angels
Afternoons to play.
I met one,—forgot my school-mates,
All, for him, straightway.

God calls home the angels promptly
At the setting sun;
I missed mine. How dreary marbles,
After playing Crown!

Emily Dickinson

Angels

How shall we tell an angel
From another guest?
How, from the common worldly herd,
One of the blest?

Hint of suppressed halo,
Rustle of hidden wings,
Wafture of heavenly frankincense,—
Which of these things?

The old Sphinx smiles so subtly:
'I give no golden rule,—
Yet would I warn thee, World: treat well
Whom thou call'st fool.'

Gertrude Hall

Adsum

The angel came by night
(Such angels still come down),
And like a winter cloud
Passed over London town;

Along its lonesome streets,
Where Want had ceased to weep,
Until it reached a house
Where a great man lay asleep;

The man of all his time
Who knew the most of men,
The soundest head and heart,
The sharpest, kindest pen.

It paused beside his bed,
And whispered in his ear;
He never turned his head,
But answered, 'I am here.'

Into the night they went.
At morning, side by side,
They gained the sacred Place
Where the greatest Dead abide.

Where grand old Homer sits
In godlike state benign;
Where broods in endless thought
The awful Florentine;

Where sweet Cervantes walks,
A smile on his grave face;
Where gossips quaint Montaigne,
The wisest of his race;

Where Goethe looks through all
With that calm eye of his;
Where—little seen but Light—
The only Shakespeare is!

When the new Spirit came,
They asked him, drawing near,
'Art thou become like us?'
He answered, 'I am here.'

Richard Henry Stoddard

Dawn Angels

All night I watched awake for morning,
At last the East grew all aflame,
The birds for welcome sang, or warning,
And with their singing morning came.

Along the gold-green heavens drifted
Pale wandering souls that shun the light,
Whose cloudy pinions, torn and rifted,
Had beat the bars of Heaven all night.

These clustered round the moon, but higher
A troop of shining spirits went,
Who were not made of wind or fire,
But some divine dream-element.

Some held the Light, while those remaining
Shook out their harvest-colored wings,
A faint unusual music raining,
 (Whose sound was Light) on earthly things.

They sang, and as a mighty river
Their voices washed the night away,
From East to West ran one white shiver,
And waxen strong their song was Day.

Agnes Mary Frances Darmesteter

Footsteps of Angels

When the hours of Day are numbered,
And the voices of the Night
Wake the better soul, that slumbered,
To a holy, calm delight;

Ere the evening lamps are lighted,
And, like phantoms grim and tall,
Shadows from the fitful firelight
Dance upon the parlour wall;

Then the forms of the departed
Enter at the open door;
The beloved, the true-hearted,
Come to visit me once more;

He, the young and strong, who cherished
Noble longings for the strife,
By the roadside fell and perished,
Weary with the march of life!

They, the holy ones and weakly,
Who the cross of suffering bore,
Folded their pale hands so meekly,
Spake with us on earth no more!

And with them the Being Beauteous,
Who unto my youth was given,
More than all things else to love me,
And is now a saint in heaven.

With a slow and noiseless footstep
Comes that messenger divine,
Takes the vacant chair beside me,
Lays her gentle hand in mine.

And she sits and gazes at me
 With those deep and tender eyes,
Like the stars, so still and saint-like,
Looking downward from the skies

Uttered not, yet comprehended,
Is the spirit's voiceless prayer,
Soft rebukes, in blessings ended,
Breathing from her lips of air.

Oh, though oft depressed and lonely,
All my fears are laid aside,
If I but remember only
Such as these have lived and died!

Henry Wadsworth Longfellow

While Loveliness Goes By

Sometimes when all the world seems grey and dun
And nothing beautiful, a voice will cry,
'Look out, look out! Angels are drawing nigh!'
Then my slow burdens leave me one by one,
And swiftly does my heart arise and run
Even like a child while loveliness goes by—
And common folk seem children of the sky,
And common things seem shapèd of the sun.
Oh, pitiful! that I who love them, must
So soon perceive their shining garments fade!
And slowly, slowly, from my eyes of trust
Their flaming banners sink into a shade!
While this earth's sunshine seems the golden dust
Slow settling from that radiant cavalcade.

Anna Hempstead Branch.

Antiphon For The Angels

Spirited light! on the edge
Of the Presence your yearning
Burns in the secret darkness,
O angels, insatiably
Into God's gaze.
Perversity
Could not touch your beauty;
You are essential joy.
But your lost companion,
Angel of the crooked
Wings - he sought the summit,
Shot down the depths of God
And plummeted past Adam -
That a mud - bound spirit might soar.

Hildegard Von Bingen

The Angel's Whisper

(An old Irish belief was that when a child smiled in its sleep it was 'talking with angels.')

A baby was sleeping;
Its mother was weeping;
For her husband was far on the wild raging sea;
And the tempest was swelling
Round the fisherman's dwelling;
And she cried, 'Dermot, darling! O come back to me!'

Her beads while she numbered
The baby still slumbered,
And smiled in her face as she bended her knee:
'O, blessed be that warning,
My child, thy sleep adorning,—
For I know that the angels are whispering with thee.

'And while they are keeping
Bright watch o'er thy sleeping,
O, pray to them softly, my baby, with me,—
And say thou wouldst rather
They 'd watch o'er thy father!
For I know that the angels are whispering with thee.'

The dawn of the morning
Saw Dermot returning,
And the wife wept with joy her babe's father to see;
And closely caressing
Her child with a blessing,
Said, 'I knew that the angels were whispering with thee.'

Samuel Lover

The Angel's Kiss

An angel stood beside the bed
Where lay the living and the dead.
He gave the mother — her who died —
A kiss that Christ the Crucified

Had sent to greet the weary soul
When, worn and faint, it reached its goal.

He gave the infant kisses twain,
One on the breast, one on the brain.

'Go forth into the world,' he said,
'With blessings on your heart and head,

'For God, who ruleth righteously,
Hath ordered that to such as be

'From birth deprived of mother's love,
I bring His blessing from above;

'But if the mother's life he spare
Then she is made God's messenger

'To kiss and pray that heart and brain
May go through life without a stain.'

The infant moved towards the light,
The angel spread his wings in flight.

But each man carries to his grave
The kisses that in hopes to save
The angel or his mother gave.

Banjo Paterson

An Angel In The House

How sweet it were, if without feeble fright,
Or dying of the dreadful beauteous sight,
An angel came to us, and we could bear
To see him issue from the silent air
At evening in our room, and bend on ours
His divine eyes, and bring us from his bowers
News of dear friends, and children who have never
Been dead indeed, — as we shall know forever.
Alas! we think not what we daily see
About our hearths, — angels that are to be,
Or may be if they will, and we prepare
Their souls and ours to meet in happy air; —
A child, a friend, a wife whose soft heart sings
In unison with ours, breeding its future wings.

James Henry Leigh Hunt

I Heard An Angel

I heard an Angel singing
When the day was springing,
'Mercy, Pity, Peace
Is the world's release.'

Thus he sung all day
Over the new mown hay,
Till the sun went down
And haycocks looked brown.

I heard a Devil curse
Over the heath and the furze,
'Mercy could be no more,
If there was nobody poor,

And pity no more could be,
If all were as happy as we.'
At his curse the sun went down,
And the heavens gave a frown.

Down pour'd the heavy rain
Over the new reap'd grain ...
And Miseries' increase
Is Mercy, Pity, Peace.

William Blake

Two Loves I Have, Of Comfort And Despair

Two loves I have, of comfort and despair,
Which like two spirits do suggest me still:
The better angel is a man right fair,
The worser spirit a woman coloured ill.
To win me soon to hell, my female evil
Tempteth my better angel from my side,
And would corrupt my saint to be a devil,
Wooing his purity with her foul pride.
And whether that my angel be turned fiend,
Suspect I may, yet not directly tell;
But being both from me both to each friend,
I guess one angel in another's hell.
Yet this shall I ne'er know, but live in doubt,
Till my bad angel fire my good one out.

William Shakespeare

Two or three angels

Two or three angels
Came near to the earth.
They saw a fat church.
Little black streams of people
Came and went in continually.
And the angels were puzzled
To know why the people went thus,
And why they stayed so long within.

Stephen Crane

Life

A poor torn heart, a tattered heart,
That sat it down to rest,
Nor noticed that the ebbing day
Flowed silver to the west,
Nor noticed night did soft descend
Nor constellation burn,
Intent upon the vision
Of latitudes unknown.

The angels, happening that way,
This dusty heart espied;
Tenderly took it up from toil
And carried it to God.
There,—sandals for the barefoot;
There,—gathered from the gales,
Do the blue havens by the hand
Lead the wandering sails.

Emily Dickinson

Time and Eternity

She died,—this was the way she died;
And when her breath was done,
Took up her simple wardrobe
And started for the sun.

Her little figure at the gate
The angels must have spied,
Since I could never find her
Upon the mortal side.

Emily Dickinson

From **The Watchers**

Beside a stricken field I stood;
On the torn turf, on grass and wood,
Hung heavily the dew of blood.

Still in their fresh mounds lay the slain,
But all the air was quick with pain
And gusty sighs and tearful rain.

Two angels, each with drooping head
And folded wings and noiseless tread,
Watched by that valley of the dead.

The one, with forehead saintly bland
And lips of blessing, not command,
Leaned, weeping, on her olive wand.

The other's brows were scarred and knit,
His restless eyes were watch-fires lit,
His hands for battle-gauntlets fit.

But round me, like a silver bell
Rung down the listening sky to tell
Of holy help, a sweet voice fell.

'Still hope and trust,' it sang; 'the rod
Must fall, the wine-press must be trod,
But all is possible with God!'

John Greenleaf Whittier

Little Breeches

I don't go much on religion,
I never ain't had no show;
But I 've got a middlin' tight grip, sir,
On the handful o' things I know.
I don't pan out on the prophets   5
And free-will and that sort of thing,—
But I b'lieve in God and the angels,
Ever sence one night last spring.

I come into town with some turnips,
And my little Gabe come along,—
No four-year-old in the county
Could beat him for pretty and strong,—
Peart and chipper and sassy,
Always ready to swear and fight,—
And I 'd larnt him to chaw terbacker
Jest to keep his milk-teeth white.

The snow come down like a blanket
As I passed by Taggart's store;
I went in for a jug of molasses
And left the team at the door.
They scared at something and started,—
I heard one little squall,
And hell-to-split over the prairie
Went team, Little Breeches, and all

Hell-to-split over the prairie!
I was almost froze with skeer;
But we rousted up some torches,
And sarched for 'em far and near.
At last we struck hosses and wagon,
Snowed under a soft white mound,
Upsot, dead beat,—but of little Gabe
No hide nor hair was found.

And here all hope soured on me
Of my fellow-critter's aid;—
I jest flopped down on my marrow-bones,
Crotch-deep in the snow, and prayed.
By this, the torches was played out,
And me and Isrul Parr
Went off for some wood to a sheepfold
That he said was somewhar thar.

We found it at last, and a little shed
Where they shut up the lambs at night.
We looked in and seen them huddled thar,
So warm and sleepy and white;
And thar sot Little Breeches and chirped,
As peart as ever you see,
'I want a chaw of terbacker,
And that 's what 's the matter of me.'

How did he git thar? Angels.
He could never have walked in that storm:
They jest scooped down and toted him
To whar it was safe and warm.
And I think that saving a little child,
And fotching him to his own,
Is a derned sight better business
Than loafing around The Throne.

John Hay

My Guide

She leads me on through storm and calm,
My glorious Angel girt with light;
By dazzling isles of tropic balm,
By coasts of ice in northern night.
Now far amid the mountain shades
Her footprints gleam like golden fire,
And now adown the leafy glades
I chase the music of her lyre.

And now amid the tangled pines
That darkly robe the gorgeous steep
She beckons where in woven lines
The sunbeams through the darkness creep,
And shows in glimpses far below
The champaign stretching leagues away,
Fair cities veil'd in summer's glow
Or sparkling in the cloudless ray.

At times on seas with tempest loud,
The pilot of my bark, she stands,
And, through the rifts of driving cloud,
To tranquil bays of bounteous lands,
The grassy creek, the bowery shore,
The fringe of many a charmed realm,
She steers me safe by magic lore,
Her white arm leaning on the helm.

When, sick at heart and worn, mine eyes
I bend to earth in long despair,
She lifts her finger to the skies,
The violet deeps of lucid air,
The myriad myriad orbs that roll
In endless throngs in living space,
And all the vision of her soul
Is mirror'd in her radiant face.

George Francis Savage-Armstrong

27

The Weaver of Souls

Who is this unseen messenger
For ever between me and her,
Who brings love's precious merchandise,
The golden breath, the dew of sighs,
And the wild, gentle thoughts that dwell
Too fragile for the lips to tell,
Each at their birth, to us before
A heaving of the heart is o'er?
Who art thou, unseen messenger?

I think, O Angel of the Lord,
You make our hearts to so accord
That those who hear in after hours
May sigh for love as deep as ours;
And seek the magic that can give
An Eden where the soul may live,
Nor need to walk a road of clay
With stumbling feet, nor fall away
From thee, O Angel of the Lord.

George William Russell

Are they not all Ministering Spirits?

We see them not—we cannot hear
The music of their wing—
Yet know we that they sojourn near,
The Angels of the spring!

They glide along this lovely ground
When the first violet grows;
Their graceful hands have just unbound
The zone of yonder rose.

I gather it for thy dear breast,
From stain and shadow free:
That which an Angel's touch hath blest
Is meet, my love, for thee!

Robert Stephen Hawker

The Fallen Star

A star is gone! a star is gone!
There is a blank in Heaven;
One of the cherub choir has done
His airy course this even.

He sat upon the orb of fire
That hung for ages there,
And lent his music to the choir
That haunts the nightly air.

But when his thousand years are pass'd,
With a cherubic sigh
He vanish'd with his car at last,
For even cherubs die!

Hear how his angel-brothers mourn—
The minstrels of the spheres—
Each chiming sadly in his turn
And dropping splendid tears.

The planetary sisters all
Join in the fatal song,
And weep this hapless brother's fall,
Who sang with them so long.

But deepest of the choral band
The Lunar Spirit sings,
And with a bass-according hand
Sweeps all her sullen strings.

From the deep chambers of the dome
Where sleepless Uriel lies,
His rude harmonic thunders come
Mingled with mighty sighs.

The thousand car-bourne cherubim,
The wandering eleven,
All join to chant the dirge of him
Who fell just now from Heaven.

George Darley

She Came and Went

As a twig trembles, which a bird
Lights on to sing, then leaves unbent,
So is my memory thrilled and stirred;—
I only know she came and went.

As clasps some lake, by gusts unriven,
The blue dome's measureless content,
So my soul held that moment's heaven;—
I only know she came and went.

As, at one bound, our swift spring heaps
The orchards full of bloom and scent,
So clove her May my wintry sleeps;—
  I only know she came and went.

An angel stood and met my gaze,
Through the low doorway of my tent;
The tent is struck, the vision stays;—
I only know she came and went.

Oh, when the room grows slowly dim,
And life's last oil is nearly spent,
One gush of light these eyes will brim,
Only to think she came and went.

James Russell Lowell

The Angels' Song

It came upon the midnight clear,
That glorious song of old,
From angels bending near the earth
To touch their harps of gold:
'Peace to the earth, good-will to men
From heaven's all-gracious King!'
The world in solemn stillness lay
To hear the angels sing.

Still through the cloven skies they come,
With peaceful wings unfurled;
And still their heavenly music floats
O'er all the weary world:
Above its sad and lowly plains
They bend on heavenly wing,
And ever o'er its Babel sounds
The blessed angels sing.

Yet with the woes of sin and strife
The world has suffered long;
Beneath the angel-strain have rolled
Two thousand years of wrong;
And man, at war with man, hears not
The love-song which they bring:
O, hush the noise, ye men of strife,
And hear the angels sing!

And ye, beneath life's crushing load
Whose forms are bending low;
Who toil along the climbing way
With painful steps and slow,—
Look now! for glad and golden hours
Come swiftly on the wing;
O, rest beside the weary road,
And hear the angels sing.

For lo! the days are hastening on,
By prophet-bards foretold,
When with the ever-circling years
Comes round the age of gold;
When Peace shall over all the earth
Its ancient splendours fling,
And the whole world send back the song
Which now the angels sing.

Edmund Hamilton Sears

Around the throne of God a band

Around the throne of God a band
Of bright and glorious angels stand;
Sweet harps within their hands they hold,
And on their heads are crowns of gold.

Some wait around Him ready still
To sing His praise and do His will,
And some, when He commands them, go
To guard His servants here below.

Lord, give Thine angels every day
Command to guard us on our way,
And bid them every evening keep
Their watch around us while we sleep.

So shall no wicked thing draw near
To do us harm or cause us fear;
And we shall dwell, when life is past,
With angels round Thy throne at last.

John M Neale

Thy wingèd troops, O God of hosts!

Thy wingèd troops, O God of hosts!
Wait on Thy wandering church below:
Here we are sailing to Thy coasts;
Let angels be our convoy, too.

Are they not all Thy servants, Lord?
At Thy command they go and come;
With cheerful haste obey Thy word,
And guard Thy children to their home.

Isaac Watts

O ye immortal throng

O ye immortal throng of angels round the throne,
Join with our feeble song, to make the Saviour known:
On earth ye knew His wondrous grace;
His glorious face in Heav'n ye view.

The warbling notes pursue, and louder anthems raise,
While mortals sing with you their own Redeemer's praise:
And thou, my heart, with equal flame,
And joy the same, perform thy part.

Philip Doddridge

Other books from Montpelier Publishing available through Amazon

Body, Mind and Spirit

Non-Religious Wedding Readings
The Simple Living Companion
Non-Religious Funeral Readings
Marriage Advice
How to be Happy

Frugal living

Frontier Frugal
A Treasury of Thrift
The Men's Guide to Frugal Grooming
1001 Ways to Save Money
Gardening Tips
The Frugal Gentleman

Humour and puzzles

Wedding Jokes
The Book of Church Jokes
After Dinner Laughs
After Dinner Laughs 2
Scottish Jokes
A Little Book of Limericks
The Bumper Book of Riddles, Puzzles and Rhymes
Welsh Jokes

Men's Interest

The Pipe Smoker's Companion
Advice to Gentlemen
The Real Ale Companion
The Cigar Collection

Travel

The Dalai Lama Next Door
The Slow Bicycle Companion
Poems of London